How to Redeem Your Time Effectively

In Scriptures Light

Ngozi Muoneke

Copyright © 2016 by Ngozi Muoneke

All rights reserved. No part of this publication may be reproduced, distributed or transmitted in any form by any means, including photocopying, recording or other electronic or mechanical methods, without the prior written permission of the publisher, except in brief quotations embodied in critical reviews and certain non-l uses permitted by copyright law. For permission requests, write to the author at the address provided.

Disclaimer: This publication is designed to provide the reader educational insights and personal experience information in regard to the subject matter. It is sold with the understanding that it is your legal right to use the information; the author and publisher assume no 'responsibility' for your actions.

ISBN-13: 978-1978033900

DEDICATION

I dedicate this book to those who struggle with time management, juggle multiple responsibilities, and feel like your life is full of challenges you can't keep up with and for those who desire to manage their time in a profound and biblical way.

Also in addition, I dedicate this book to my wonderful children Gordon, Jeremiah, Marvin and Marachi who are my inspiration. To my first grand-daughter Levi who has brought me so much joy. To my wonderful daughter-in-law Zee thank you for taking care of them. To my husband Victor thank you for all you have done for us.
I Love you all!!

"Time management is a booming business everyone wants to get more done and control time wasters. But for Christians the need to manage time is even more urgent."

– Mike Bennett

CONTENTS

	Foreword	Pg. 1
1	A 24/7 Fast-Paced World?	Pg. 11
2	Why Manage Time?	Pg. 22
3	God on Time Management	Pg. 33
4	Keys to Effective Time Management	Pg. 42
	About the Author	
	References	

ACKNOWLEDGMENTS

To my Heavenly Father, I give you all the thanks and praise for your mercy and grace because with you truly all things are possible.

To my amazing dad James and siblings Joan, Doreen and Charles, all my nieces and nephews, cousins and the rest of my family around the world I love you all.

To my spiritual parents of 18 years. Rev. Pastor Thomas & Pastor Mrs. Eunice Alamu and family from Hope Assembly Ministries London. I appreciate and love you. Thank you for your love, guidance, prayers and support.

To my bestie for life of over 30 years Jackie. Thank you for being you. For all the wonderful memories over the years. I love you and am proud to call you my sister.

To Mavis Amankwah multiple award-winning entrepreneur, CEO "Rich Visons", "Be Mogul" and "Women Like Me Business Club" thank you for your invaluable advice, support, encouragement and prayers especially during challenging times and helping me gain a platform.

To Her Excellency Dr. Justina Mutale. A massive thank you and appreciation for writing such an admirable Foreword. I know how busy you are, especially with your many engagements. I am very humbled and honored.

To renowned International Speaker Dr. Donald E. Wetmore, from USA. Author of "Beat the Clock" and many more. Thank you for guidance whilst writing this book and your rapid response to my emails.

To Tina Fayemi, thanks for all our prayers and encouragement and standing by me through difficult times and understanding my vision.

To Pastor Anthony Brathwaite and Pastor Enoch Alamu I appreciate all your prayers and encouragement.

To Mr & Mrs James & Grace Olawale, Evangelist Akinrin & Family and Mr. Hezekiah Adesomi & family. Thanks for all your prayers!

To Jackson Ogunyemi (Action Jackson), CEO "The Fix Up Team" for inspiring me to take "small easy steps".

To my dear brother in Christ, Mr. Olafusi Benjamin Meroyi & family. Thank you for all your encouraging words, for keeping me in check and rebuking me even though sometimes it was hard.

To all my friends and colleagues, I appreciate you all and God bless!!

How To Redeem Your Time Effectively

This is a much-needed book for this generation where knowledge has increased in accordance with Biblical prophecy. Daniel 12:4. Her Excellency, Ambassador Dr Justina Mutale in her forward to this book has highlighted the busy times and has given her full recommendation to this book as a must read by everyone. I also give my full 100% support to this book as a 'Must Read' by everyone. There is time for everything under heaven. Eccl.3:1-8.

This is the right timing for this book to be written when we need to know how to manage our time by redeeming it, because the days are evil. Eph.5:16. I must congratulate Ngozi for her practical management of time in writing this book, you are truly a blessing to our generation.

Rev. Thomas Alamu, Senior Pastor
Hope Assembly Ministries
London, United Kingdom

FOREWORD

By Her Excellency, Ambassador Dr Justina Mutale

Franklin Benjamin, one of the founding fathers of the United States of America once said, *"never leave for tomorrow what can be done today"*. Now more than ever before, we find ourselves procrastinating and running around in circles due to unnecessary distractions on our time. The 21st Century brings with it a very fast-paced world, where everyone is running around trying to do too many things at any given time. This book comes at a time when the onset of new technologies and smart phones have made time management unmanageable and complicated. Nowadays, one usually finds unprecedented demands on one's time, with our attention being sought from all corners of the world, in different directions, day and night via smart phones with their apps and social media. Phone calls rain on you via mobile phone, landline phone, home phones, office phones, WhatsApp calls, and Facebook Messenger. In addition, there is Facetime, Instagram, and various other social media and online tools of communication, through which information and messages are relayed to us 24 hours a day. And most of this communication almost always appears to be urgent or to demand our urgent attention.

It may therefore, often seem that there isn't enough time in a day to do everything that one needs to do. This false perspective on time can lead to a build-up of unnecessary stress. Now more than ever, is the time to invest in time management skills. Managing one's time is valuable in all spheres of our lives, whether it be work, family or leisure. It is important that we develop effective strategies for managing our time to balance the conflicting demands on our time. Once we have identified ways in which we can improve the management of our time, we can begin to adjust our routines and patterns of behaviour to reduce any time-related stress in our lives.

Ngozi Muoneke is qualified to talk and write about time management through her training, as well as work and life experiences. As co-owner of a cosmetics company, Ngozi is an accomplished Cosmetic Formulator, Entrepreneur, Mentor, Author and Public Speaker. She is also a wife, mother and homemaker with four children.

Ngozi utilises her extensive skills and experience in the pharmaceutical and cosmetic industry to formulate and manufacture skincare, hair care and personal care products for African/Caribbean skin types. Her products are widely sought after in the Caribbean Islands, South America, USA, Africa and other parts of the world. In addition to managing time for her family commitments, time to her husband and children of varying ages, Ngozi also has to manage time for her production staff and management team and running her company. Furthermore, she has to manage time and her relationships with her suppliers and clients in a global market. Managing all these relations and transactions requires great expertise at time management.

I was in the process of preparing for the Women in Trade (WINTRADE) Global Convention in London, when Ngozi approached me to write the Foreword for this book. And I thought, how timely that this request should come at a time when I am trying to fight for time to do some many things at the same time. WINTRADE Week took place over a period of 5 days with 12 events held at 10 venues across London, attracting over 200 women entrepreneurs from across the globe. You can imagine just how much time was involved in organising this event, and just how time management was of utmost importance to get the WITRADE Week on track, while communicating with people from different time zones and working out the timetable for the various WINTRADE events to run smoothly according to the set time across London.

In this book, Ngozi shares her expertise and outlines some of the skills required to manage your time, including setting clear goals, breaking your goals down into discreet steps, and reviewing your progress towards your goals. Other skills involved include prioritising and focusing on urgent and important tasks rather than those that are not important or don't move you towards your goals; organising your work schedule; list making to remind you of what you need to do when; persevering when things are not working out and avoiding procrastination.

It has been often said that *"timing is everything"*. Therefore, choosing an opportune moment to do something always has an impact as to whether that undertaking will succeed or fail. In some cultures, it is believed that planting a seed during the full moon, guarantees a big harvest. This also applies to success when starting at new job or simply embarking a new adventure, new endeavour or indeed even a new relationship in one's social life. Earlier in the year, I had attended the 61st Session of the United Nations Commission on the Status of Women (UN-CSW61) held at the United Nations Headquarters in New York, under the priority theme of *"Women's Economic Empowerment in a Changing World of Work"*.

It therefore, followed that planning WINTRADE Week was timely as it responded directly to the UNCSW61 theme, of empowering women through international trade.

In asking me to do this Foreword, Ngozi pointed out to me that she believed that I was good at managing my time as I have so many responsibilities and demands on my time that span the globe. I serve as Founding Partner, President, Patron, Ambassador, Advisor, Board Member, Consultant and Mentor to various commercial, humanitarian, charitable and community organisations in the UK and overseas, in addition to being an International Keynote Speaker with speaking engagements lined-up across the globe. Many people wonder how I manage to do what I do given that there are only 24 hours in a day. I am often asked where I get the energy and time to be able to honour my commitments in different parts of the world.

My attitude to time is guided by the understanding that there is a difference between *"Clock Time"* and *"Real Time"*, as stated by Mathews J. et al in the *Entrepreneurs*. I believe that if one cannot tell the difference between the two, then everything else that one might try to do to manage one's time will not work to one's benefit. To begin with, before one can even think of managing one's time, one must learn, recognise, and understand what time really is. As defined by the English Dictionary time is *"the point or period at which things occur."* This means that time is when events take place. Time is that point at which you take action. It is the moment in which you do things. Therefore, time is not before, neither is it after. It is important to always bear in mind that there are two types of time. It is common knowledge that in clock time, we have 60 seconds in a minute, 60 minutes in an hour, 24 hours in a day and 365 days in a year. Therefore, all time passes equally in *Clock Time*. However, time is relative in *Real Time*. You will find that in real time, time flies or drags depending on what you're doing. Two hours waiting to board a flight can feel like 10 years if you are in a hurry to get to your destination. And yet a 10-year-old child may appear to have grown up in just two hours. In trying to manage time, you must decide which time describes the world in which you live.

The reason that many people fail to manage their time is that they live in clock time, which is irrelevant when it comes to managing your time. In a fast-paced world, you don't live in, or even have access to clock time. You have to live in real time, a world in which all time flies when you are enjoying what you are doing or drags when you are doing what you do not enjoy doing. In real time, you create your own time and you manage it according to what needs to be done. By so doing, you can remove any self-sabotage or self-limitation based around the notion of *"not having enough time,"*.

Regardless of the type of field that you work in, your work will be composed of three main items: Ideas, Conversations and Actions. It is only natural that you may be frequently interrupted or pulled in different directions. However, when you live in real time, you get to decide how much time you spend on those interruptions and how much time you spend on the thoughts, conversations and actions that will lead you to success, even though you cannot eliminate the frequent interruptions.

This book is a must-read for anyone who finds themselves running around in circles trying to find time to do things. If you have been struggling with your time in this fast-paced world, the tips provided by Ngozi in this book will help you to effortlessly utilise your time and effectively strategize and prioritise your real time in order to get the best out of your time. Despite living in a fast-paced world, when you follow Ngozi's tips and try to live in real time, you will realise just how much more effortless your life can be when you don't have to waste the time that you have, doing things that drain your energy as opposed to those that give you back the energy to venture forth. This book is your ultimate guide to redeeming your time effectively and effortlessly.

Her Excellency Ambassador Dr Justina Mutale
Multi-Award Winning African Woman of the Year
Vice-Chancellor, Excel Research University
Founder & President, Justina Mutale Foundation for Leadership
Founder, POSITIVE RUNWAY: Global Catwalk to Stop the Spread (of HIVAIDS)
Gender Equality Ambassador & Spokesperson, International Women's Think Tank
Advisory Board Member, World Leaders Forum
More info: www.justinamutale.com

NGOZI MUONEKE

CHAPTER 1

A 24/7 FAST-PACED WORLD?

Have you ever wondered why there never seems to be enough time? If I only had another hour, half an hour, or five minutes, we sometimes groan, knowing all too well that there are 24 hours each day, and that this will not change no matter how much we desire it to change.

I'm a wife, mother, grandmother, multiple-award-winning entrepreneur, and active leader in my local church. I lead a pretty busy life, and still have to manage everything and everyone in my life. How?, you may ask. Well, I often get asked how I manage to get so much done. As a Christian, it is essential for me to be able to manage my time, as our Earthly sojourn is significantly shorter than we may be inclined to think. 'You have made my days a mere handbreadth; the span of my years is as nothing before you. Each man's life is but a breath, - *Psalm 39:4-5*.

There must be balance. I remember occasions, depending on which project I was working on, where I would go 24 hours without sleep or having a proper dinner. At the time, I felt quite proud of myself for being able to do this, and of the fact that at the end of the day, I had been able to complete my projects. But then I would spend the next few days not knowing if I was coming or going. I soon realized that it was not so wise after all. Remember that you and your health are important.

'Teach us to number our days, that we may gain a heart of wisdom, - *Psalm 90:12*. In this fast paced, 24/7 world, there just never seems to be enough time. Even if you decide to spend valuable family time with family or friends and decide to go out for a meal, while you're waiting to be served, some of your family members will be engrossed with their smart phones or with Facebook, totally oblivious to the fact that it's meant to be family time,

that means talking to each other, catching up, and enjoying each other's company. Maybe you have seen the same thing, too, perhaps even in your own family. When I am asked how I manage my time, I simply say, 'in small easy steps,' a phrase from I learned from motivational speaker and CEO Fixup Enterprise, Jackson Ogunyemi better known as 'Action Jackson'. I was really inspired when I first heard him speak. It's all about sacrifice. A typical day starts around 5am, with prayer and cooking lunch, be it potatoes or pasta, and whilst that is cooking, I run the shower or bath. By the end of my bath, lunch is ready, and after I get ready for work, which runs from 8:30am–5pm. I get home around 6pm, and prepare the family meal by 7pm. Around 9pm, when the family has gone to bed, I usually work on my other projects, that is, products, designing labels, etc. Before I go to bed, which is usually in the early hours of the morning, I ensure that

I pray and read my Bible. My quiet time with the Lord is so important to me, including my prayer life, and it doesn't matter if I'm on the bus, train, or at work and during my tea breaks, including toilet breaks, I will find time to pray. I plan my day according to the stages of my day by minimizing distractions. For example, if interrupted at work, I kindly ask not to be disturbed until I have completed a task. Most of the time, when I'm working on projects, the television is on as background noise, but if a program catches my attention, I mute the television so as not to be distracted from what I'm doing. It took time to discipline myself to manage my time in an effective manner that enabled me to see great results.

We live in a generation with always-on access to global news, information, and even to other people. To lose focus has become a normal thing. Either we are constantly flipping channels, or we start to treat our attention like currency, meticulously refusing to spend it all in one place. We hardly have a grasp of what is most important to us, things we should let go and let be, and what should either take precedence or lots of our attention and time.

In a nutshell, many people are living according to the dictates and demands of this fast-paced generation without any plan or scheme put in place to have it under control instead. Our efficiency is in having this dispensation serve us, instead of being its servant—controlled, swayed, and employed by the alluring distractions of new technologies, and instructed by the irresponsible and time-wasting habits that they cause.

This is has become an extremely fast-paced world. It has subsequently become easy, if not 'normal', to live as though playing catch up with time all the time. Demanding jobs, the strive for self-sustenance, and struggles for life balance, among many other things, have a way of making people activities-conscious, and people become silly managers of time and self along the way. It is increasingly common to have more and more activities cramped into an already-congested to-do list of what is probably neither important nor necessary.

One thing that has changed is our focus. Focus is what helps us to pick our priorities and to have a grasp of what is most essential to pursue, instantly or not. In our today's culture, it is quite normal for people to be distracted and rarely fully present. That is why we must really fight against getting pulled into the orbit of that always-constant gravity of busyness. Focus is almost dead. Concentration is strangulated. Decisiveness has been ground in the mill. Urgent tasks and priorities, even though we recognize them, are desperate voices for our attention. The stresses that we often undergo doing those other tasks we claim we 'have to do' don't always measure up to the pain that the voices of those legitimate priorities do to our well-being.

In the cloud of endless to-dos at work, home, church, club, gym etc., our minds are so cluttered that we even overlook simple matters like the joy of being alive today. And, now, be honest with me: since you have started reading this little piece, do your thoughts stay concentrated, or do they try to wander to something else happening in your life, or it has even done so in the first place?

A day holds a lot of time: 24 hours. 1,440 minutes. 86,400 seconds. Isn't that a lot of time? Never mind.

Richard Branson and Mark Zuckerberg have the same amount of time—24 hours, the same as you, I, and the most unfulfilled person you can point to. Yet for most of us, our daily cry is, 'If only I had more time!' We all feel so busy—overwhelmed by our lengthy and never-ending to-do lists.

Busyness has become a status symbol in the United States, United Kingdom, Asia, and Africa, anywhere and everywhere. It is the official language of most people in this fast-paced generation. Even we as Christians fall into the trap of over-scheduling, over-doing, and over-committing our time and resources. It has become more about 'doing' than 'fulfilling'. Good time management requires an important shift in our focus, from activities to results: being busy isn't the same as being effective.

The earlier-mentioned scenario of the family meal is a lucid depiction of what our time-valuing habits and time management culture have become. We now spend more time on our smartphones than with our partner, according to a new study. While the average smartphone user tends to spend two hours a day on his or her phone, the average amount of time we spend with our partners per day is just 97 minutes.

I don't think it is really important to ask if the time we spend online and on our phones is worth it, if it means the actualization and fulfillment of something definitive in regards to personal and professional goals. I think we all know the answer. That is what we have woken up to, and have come to see. 'Time management' is the process of organizing and planning how to divide your time between specific activities. Good time management enables you to work smarter—not harder—so that you can get more done in less time, even when time is tight and pressures are high. Failing to manage your time damages your effectiveness and causes stress.

The Gone-Are-The-Days Strategies

Of course, we have always managed time, but just like any strategy or technology, what worked mere short years ago may be totally obsolete and irrelevant later. Traditional time management strategies have become too limited in today's fast-paced, complex world. Technology has allowed us to be more mobile and always connected.

Many don't have regular 'traditional' office hours, and many don't even need an office at all. All these aspects can really make it difficult to have an accurate schedule.

Shall we bring some classic time-management advice into the 21st century to see how it fits?

'Either professionally or personally, eliminating the "unnecessary" in life goes a long way in making you more productive. What do I consider unnecessary? Well, strictly speaking, anything that prevents you from reaching your particular goal. If your goal is to learn a new language, or read a book then don't spend 45 minutes on social media. If you have a deadline to make at work, don't spend 25 minutes per day fielding unnecessary phone calls. Put simply, you need to draw a firm, distinct line between the "necessary" and "unnecessary" in your life'. David Bakke, *Money Crashers*.

Whatever Is Worth Doing Is Worth Doing Well

The truth remains that there is nothing wrong with wanting to unleash your absolute best on a particular project, but in this fast-paced society, the luxury of large blocks of time to devote to an assignment is no longer available. A better strategy now is to break the project into tasks that can be done in smaller segments of time. When you work on a project consistently over time in small doses, rather than waiting for the perfect circumstance in which to attack it once and for all, there is a greater chance that the project will be a job well-done. Perfectionism is a stumbling block for productivity.

Follow a Daily Plan

This doesn't work for everyone. Now, many workers aren't in the same place on the same day each week. There are emerging programs and apps that give us detailed information that we need for our projects anywhere we are. Our focus in this fast-paced world should be on task-management instead of time-management. It is largely unrealistic that we will touch a piece of paper only 'once'. The best strategy is to make a decision about each item as we handle it, and that can be a decision to look at it later. The idea is to keep moving forward by determining the next course of action, not touching 'some' papers once.

CHAPTER 2

WHY MANAGE TIME?

'Time is the most valuable coin in your life. You and you alone will determine how that coin will be spent. Be careful that you do not let other people spend it for you'. - **Carl Sandberg**

Why do we manage time? Or why do we have to manage time? Poor time managers and those who are effective at using their time will definitely have something to say. But would the answers explain why, despite having an equal 24 hours in a day, some achieve phenomenal things and others don't, or will it be a mere 'school' definition of time management, irrespective of personal experiences?

I think it will likely be the second option. We can all probably define time management, but we can hardly manage our time. We don't even know why time needs to be managed.

In reality, we manage time because we not only need to do more in less time, we have to. Some have mistaken time management to be cramming more stuff into an already overloaded schedule. That can never be. That is not good time management, but rather mindless choking.

The central reason we need to manage our time is because our time is limited. Imagine that you had a vault full of money that can never be exhausted, and you are assured that no matter how much you spend, there will always be more in the vault. Now, ask yourself the following questions:

What would be your spending habits? What school would your kids attend? What kind of trips and adventures wouldn't you consider, even a month or a few in the Caribbean, and another month, say, in Asia, South America, or Africa? Wouldn't you give billions to famine relief and disaster victims, and remember the orphans, homeless, and those dying from famine in different parts of the world, or even in your own community? I guess you might want to pump billions into a firm that is committed to finding a lasting solution for AIDS, diabetes and cancer? And when a research group becomes committed to eliminating Coronary Artery Disease (Ischemic Heart Disease) a disease that 7.2 million people died of in 2012, wouldn't you release trillions?

That is exactly how it is with our time. If our time were unlimited, if we could live forever and have all the time to ourselves, then we would take liberty in using the abundance of hours within our grasp to do things anytime we wanted to do them and however we wanted to do them. But since it is more than sure that we have limited time, and in that time we want to fulfill goals, achieve our ambition, and fulfill our dreams, personally, professionally, and spiritually, it becomes important to master the act of knowing how to do all we can do effectively within our limited years.

I always ask a question: If we divide the number of years we want to live on this earth into smaller equivalents, what do we get? We get hours. Let's do some simple math. If your ideal year is 70 years, that means you have a totality of 25,550 days to live on Earth, which is 613,200 hours, 36,792,000 minutes, or 2,207,520,000 seconds. That is about 2.2 billion seconds to live that must be managed! So, in a nutshell, managing our time means managing our lives. The depth of time-management is self-management. There is no great time-manager with poor personal-management skills. Both work hand in hand.

Most people live by the clock, because time is important to all of us. Benjamin Franklin said, 'Do not squander time, for it is the stuff life is made of'.

As Christians

'To have more peace, as well as more time, start by letting go of the notion that time can be manipulated. Then, let go of the idea that it confines you. Instead, set out to use the time that is there for its true and best purpose – as the space within which you can live your life to the fullest'.

— Michelle Passoff

As a Christian, just as we should remember that our money and other possessions are on loan to us from God as an instrument of good works, we should be managing our time, because it is not ours. Managing our time is very important, because God wants us to be stewards of all that He has entrusted unto us. We have been given a certain amount of time here on Earth for our lifetime. From the student at school, college or university, to the CEO of Dangote Group, we all have been given certain amount of hours to accomplish our tasks. When we manage our time effectively, we not only accomplish what is required of us, but we also find balance in all the different areas of our life.

Know that our time is our most valuable possession. *Ecclesiastes 3:1* says, 'There is a time appointed for everything and a time for every delight and event or purpose under heaven'. When Queen Elizabeth was about to die, even though she was arguably the richest woman in her lifetime, her last words were, 'I would give all my kingdom for one more moment of time'.

The average person uses 13 different methods to control and manage his or her time. The average person undergoes 1 interruption every 8 minutes, or approximately 7 interruptions per hour, which makes 50–60 interruptions per day. The average interruption takes 5 minutes, totaling about 4 hours, or 50% of the average workday. 80% of those interruptions are rated as of 'little value' or of 'no value', creating approximately 3 hours of wasted time each day. Shocking, isn't it?

When we keep a right perspective of the place of God in the discourse of time management, that is, remembering that all time belongs to Him, we will begin to see a lot of things in a different light.

In *James 4:14*, we are reminded about the nature of our life. 'What is our life? We are a mist that appears for a little while and then vanishes'. We can never have more time, but we can live with an even greater awareness of the limited time that we do have. When we make the decision to see with God's perspective the time we have in this temporal world, we will be able to enjoy each moment of our lives and live the kind of life that we want to live. Each day that is presented before us is amazing. We should not, like normal people, leave this precious gift unwrapped and unappreciated till it is gone before we realize it.

Jesus Christ's Example

Jesus had to make difficult decisions about how He spent His time on Earth, and his three years in ministry have taught us a lot of lessons. We know these lessons through the words He gave us as the Holy Scriptures. His life was a case study of choosing priorities, and choosing what is most important to do at certain times. His admonition for believers to seek first the kingdom of God in Matthew is a clear example. That is the master Himself teaching us to set the right priorities.

The Apostle Paul wrote to the church at Ephesus in *Ephesians 5:15–16*, 'Be careful, then, how you live—not as unwise but wise, making most of every opportunities'. He was telling us be discreet and astute in our decision making when beset with a difficult situation. He would write to the Colossians in *Colossians 3:17*, 'Whatever you do, whether in word or deed, do it all in the name of the Lord Jesus'. This verse reveals the importance of our time and activities to God, and hence the need to focus on things that are important to God.

Beyond focusing on just having a to-do list, we should concentrate on the purpose for which God created us. That ultimately gives us the peace to say 'no' to some good things and 'yes' to others, even if they are unconventional. Rather than just reacting and living according to the wave of things and activities that wants to draw us into actions, we can ride over them with deliberate intention and masterfully use our time on what is most important.

There are many reasons we manage time as it applies to us in a different way. Here are some:

To Say No

We manage time so that we can unleash the power of 'no'. Keeping a balance between work, home, children, husband, church, family, and friends can be a very daunting task. We must unleash a strong component of time management, saying outright 'no' to many good and genuine things because of an ulterior focus in mind. We have 24 hours each day, and to be able to do all that God wants us to do means that we must reject everything that isn't important. Each 'no' we say reflects the need for time-management. Keep in mind that every opportunity—no matter how good or helpful it may be to others—is not necessarily right for you at this moment. When things are out of control, when order and balance seem far away, the power of 'no' helps us out. So, we manage time because we must say 'no' to many things in order for our lives to take perfect shape, and so that we can accomplish more.

To Rest

One of the major reasons we manage time is so that we can have days off to rest. Jesus Christ demonstrated rest in the way He handled the Sabbath. God already established this ratio, even at creation. He prescribed six days of work and one day of rest. That isn't to say that we must work from Monday to Saturday, and rest on Sundays alone. God's act served only to establish the need to take a break after working on something meaningful and definitive in our lives. When we take appropriate rest, we have more energy to continue. This is a major reason why we manage time.

To Maximize Productivity

When we manage our time, it is a natural phenomenon that we become more productive and less stressed. Only then are we able to fulfill our destinies. Maximizing productivity means mastering time in such a way that we always have the opportunity to showcase our skills and unleash our potential to benefit the world, without having to take some of this potential to the grave. To maximize productivity is to die empty. There is a direct correlation between peak performance and time management. Peak performance is the same as 'maximum productivity'.

We manage time not only because we need to, but because we must perform at our peak personally, professionally, and in other areas of our lives. By taking 1 hour per day for independent study, which is 7 hours per week, or 365 hours in a year, one can learn at the rate of a full-time student. In 3 to 5 years, the average person can become an expert in the topic of his or her choice, by spending only one hour per day.

CHAPTER 3

GOD ON TIME MANAGEMENT

The Holy Scriptures contain over 400 verses about time, and I believe that this means that time management is of great importance to God. Every minute we spend each day is either wasted or wisely invested. God, not bound by time, created time and gave us time as stewards. In fact, the Scriptures regard how we manage time as a spiritual discipline.

Moses prayed to God in *Psalm 90:12*: 'Teach us to number our days, that we may grow in wisdom'. If we don't wisely use our time, we will find that we have little time to do what is important. We must all take responsibility for how we spend the time that God has given us. Moses's prayer shows that it takes wisdom to be able to master the shades of time management to and apply time management to our personal lives.

Every morning, we are credited with 86,400 seconds, and no balance whatsoever is carried into the next day. Every night erases what we fail to use wisely. Any time that we use inappropriately or ineffectively is lost forever, and cannot be reclaimed. Time that is used unwisely reveals our weaknesses. There are no greater and more valuable investments we can make than to set aside daily time to sit at the feet of Christ and to learn from His immense and eternal streams of wisdom.

Time is precious, but we do not know yet how precious it really is. We will only know when we are no longer able to take advantage of it. Liberal and generous in every way, God in the wise economy of His providence teaches us that we should be prudent about the proper use of time. He never gives us two moments at the same time. He never gives us a second moment without taking away the first. And He never grants us that second moment without holding the third one in His hand, leaving us completely uncertain as to whether or not we will have it.

The great saints of old learned the wisdom of having only two days on their calendars: today and *that* day (the day on which they would be with the Lord). If we want a heart of wisdom, we must learn to live each day in light of *that* day. When we daily remind ourselves of the purpose of our sojourn here on earth, we will cultivate an eternal perspective on time, and it will influence our work and all our relationships.

God's relationship to time is one of the great mysteries of the Bible. Peter tells us, 'With the Lord a day is like a thousand years, and a thousand years are like a day' (*2 Peter 3:8*). Peter seems to be recalling Moses's words: 'For a thousand years in your sight are like a day that has just gone by, or like a watch in the night' (*Psalm 90:4*). A watch lasted three hours. Imagine: a thousand years going by as if they were three hours! If a man's life lasts roughly 70 years (*Psalm 90:10*), and a thousand years is like 3 hours, then our entire lives would be reduced to 12 minutes and 36 seconds! On this scale, our entire sojourn on this earth whizzes past in a blur. We're born, we start school, we move away for college, we get a job, we get married, we have children of our own, we have grandkids, we retire, we die. And, yet, the Lord continues 'from everlasting to everlasting'. (Psalm 90:2). He is the God of time.

God's View

In America, time management is a billion-dollar industry. In almost every business in America, experts and consultants are hired to teach busy executives how to better manage their time and how to improve their performance. I used to think that time management could be a misleading concept. It begs the question: Can we truly manage time? What is, then, the meaning of 'manage', if we cannot delay time, speed it up, save it, or lose it? Time is something strictly under God's domain. Irrespective of what we do, time keeps moving forward at the same rate all the time.

Jesus Christ had to make difficult decisions about how He would spend his limited time on Earth. His example has a lot to teach us. But we must take the time to discover which things are important to God by reading the words He gave us. We must also invest time meditating on what those things mean in our everyday lives. Then, the next time the chaos of urgency tries to dictate your next action, you can press pause. Having already thought about which things are most important, you'll be able to make intentional decisions. (Urgent does not necessarily equal important.) Even if a decision carries you another step forward, it's not progress if it leads you away from where you want to go.

The challenge is not to manage time. The challenge is to manage ourselves as we determine how best to use our time.

In *Ephesians 5:16*, the Bible uses another phrase instead of 'managing our time'. It speaks of 'redeeming' our time. In *Ephesians 5:14-15*, Paul warned us to 'see then that you walk circumspectly, not as fools, but as wise, redeeming

the time because the days are evil'. What is the meaning of the phrase, *walk circumspectly*? It means to be constantly looking for every opportunity to invest our time wisely.

In light of the Scriptures and God's words, there are three basic principles of managing your time more wisely:

Set Priorities

Ecclesiastes 3:1 says, 'There is a time for everything, and a season for everything under the heavens'. There is a time to do what is important and life-defining because its season is right. There is also a time not to do it. In essence, we set our life priorities, or we allow circumstances and people to tell us what we should do or what our priorities should be.

Schedule Priorities

It is not enough only to have priorities and to cram them into a to-do list; there is a right time and a right way to go about this. *Ecclesiastes Chapter 8:5 – 6* cautions, 'For a wise heart knows the proper time and procedure, for there is a proper time and procedure for every delight'. We must schedule the right, hassle-free time to carry out those priorities.

Stick to Priorities

It is not enough to set and schedule, for every challenge will come up against it. In *Ephesians 5:16*, Paul taught us to *make the most of every opportunity*. Let your priorities stand firm in the face of change. Go all the way to carry them out. Remember, 'With the Lord a day is like a thousand years, and a thousand years are like a day' *(2 Peter 3:8)*. From that perspective, God has only waited two days since the day Jesus was born. God, literally, has all the time in the world. He's not in a hurry, nor is He taking his time. He is God, and He will do what He will do when He wills it.

Taking this idea to its logical extension, an infinitesimal moment is like eternity, and eternity is like an infinitesimal moment. This is how God can communicate with all of His children and hear all the prayers we pray simultaneously. It is part of His ability to be omnipresent. God, being everywhere at once, views all things as part of an eternal here and now. And, in each moment, He has all the 'time' He needs to provide each of us with the care that He has promised us. For Him, there is no beginning and no end, no before and no after, save in the way He chooses to communicate with us.

"He who every morning plans the transactions of that day and follows that plan carries a thread that will guide him through the labyrinth of the most busy life."
— *Victor Hugo*

CHAPTER 4

KEYS TO EFFECTIVE TIME MANAGEMENT

Charles Schwab, the president of Bethlehem Steel, hired a consultant and said to him, 'If you'll show me how I and other top managers in our company can use our time better, I will pay you a fee of whatever you ask within reason'.

The man relaxed, and said, 'All right'. He handed Schwab a blank sheet of paper and said, 'I want you to write on this sheet of paper all the important things you need to do tomorrow, and list them in order of priority. Put the most important thing you should do tomorrow as number one. Put the second most important thing you should do as number two, and so forth. When you go into work tomorrow morning, start with the first thing on your list, and stick with it until you finish it. Then move on to number two, and so forth. You may not be able to accomplish all the things on your list in one day, but you will have accomplished the most important thing on your list, or at least made a major effort. Then, tomorrow night, make a new list for the upcoming day. Do this for several weeks and let me know what happens'.

That was the basic secret, and Schwab got it. This remains the basic principle on which time management operates. There are many more very important principles that will help you master yourself and your time to get things done when they should be done.

Assume Responsibility

The first key is to assume responsibility for how you spend and use your time. It is a personal decision to be responsible for almost anything in life. That means that you take the blame for your wasted time, distractions, and the time you spend on things that are unimportant. If there is a void of leadership in your time management life, someone

will fill that void. This does not mean that others are bad people, but that others will take all of your time if you let them. You will have worked hard, but you may not have done enough of the right things. Time management is not doing the wrong things quicker. That just gets us nowhere faster. Time management is doing the right things. The Bible challenges us to redeem time, which means to make the most of the time that God has given us (see *Ephesians 5:16*). Choose to take charge of your
time to the best of your ability. If you don't manage your time, somebody else will.

Plan Your Schedule

Don't let months go by without making any progress towards the fulfillment of your God-given goals. Plan your schedule, and turn your goals and dreams into deadlines. Our lives are made up of seven vital areas: Health, Family, Finance, Intellect, Sociality, Profession, and Spirituality. We will not necessarily spend time every day in each area, or equal amounts of time in each area. But if, in the long run, we spend a sufficient quantity and quality of time in each area, our lives will be in balance.

But if we neglect any one area, never mind two or three areas, we will eventually sabotage our success. Much like a table, if one leg is longer than the rest, it will make the entire table wobbly. If we don't take time for health, our family life and social life will suffer. If our finances are out of balance, we will not be able to focus adequately on our professional goals, and so on.

You must control and organize your time effectively for maximum productivity and efficiency. Find the hours of your greatest strength and sensitivity, and pour all your effort into them, after setting those times for work directly within your timeframe. Do what works best for you. If evening is your strongest hour, pick it. If it is the middle of the night, after everyone has gone to bed, pick it!

Get Organized and Stay Organized

Remove all the clutter from your life, and ask the Lord to help you. These are things that pull you away from your dreams. These also include unimportant things, activities, and obligations that choke out the important things you should be doing. We see in many places in the Bible how things are done and maintained in an orderly fashion, for example in Exodus 40:1–16. Plan your week ahead. Take a few minutes on Saturday or Sunday and jot down what you need to accomplish each day of the coming week. Be realistic. Incorporate housework, environment tidying, shopping, job-related tasks, etc. Studies have shown that the person who works with a messy desk spends, on average, 1.5 hours per day looking for things or being distracted by things. That's 7.5 hours per week. ('Out of sight, out of mind', and the reverse is true, too, 'In sight, in mind'.) And, it's not a solid block of 1.5 hours, but a minute here, and a minute there, and like a leaky hot water faucet, drip, drip, drip, it doesn't seem like a major loss, but at the end the day, we've dumped gallons of hot water down the drain that we are paying to heat. If you have ever visited the office of a top manager, that person is typically working from a clean desk. Many would attribute this practice to that person's access to other staff members. While there may be some truth to that conclusion, in most cases, if we went back some years in that person's career, they probably were working with a clean desk back then, too, which gave them the focus they needed to be promoted to where they are today.

Eliminate the Unimportant

Remember the Charles Schwab example given above. Every night, you can start a ritual of looking at your schedule for the next day by writing your priorities down, or using an App whichever is most convenient, putting the four most important things in a priority order. The first thing you will do in the morning will be to look at it. You will carry the list with you to your work desk, and place it where you can see it. Then, the more focused you are as you see it, the greater are your chances of getting your priorities accomplished.

Beware of the time waste zone. The tendency to waste time is inborn for all of us. It could be internet surfing, chat-room discussions, Facebook and Twitter, or watching television. These aren't necessarily bad, but they can gulp time away if they aren't done with a definitive purpose in mind. Studies show that nearly 75% of us complain on a regular basis, all throughout our day, that we are flat-out tired. Most people get the correct quantity of sleep, but they lack quality of sleep. Their days are filled with so much stress, and they are so out of control, working harder but maybe not smarter, that it's difficult to get a full night's sleep. (Some simply do not allow for a sufficient quantity of sleep.) If you plan your day, then put your plan into action, you will get more done, feel a higher sense of accomplishment, experience less stress, and enjoy a more restful night's sleep.

Always Review Your Day

At the close of each day, always cultivate the habit of reviewing the way in which you have spent your time. Evaluate your schedule and ask yourself hard questions. Compare what you did that day with what you intended to do. Ask yourself: Did I make good use of my time? Did I procrastinate? Was I able to maintain my concentration and focus all through the day? Did I engage in activities that truly were priorities, or did I just fluff my day with some things that were less important? Did I make progress toward the accomplishment of my God-given goals? Did I make wise use of the time I had today?

Many do not take a lunch break, working through that time in the hope that it will give them more time to produce results. Studies have shown that this may produce just the opposite result. After working for several hours, we start to 'dull out'.

Sure, we can work through lunch and be productive, but that is not the issue.

The issue is how much more productive we can be. A lunch break, even a short 15-minute break, gives us the chance to get our batteries all charged up again so that we can more effectively handle the afternoon's challenges. We are then less likely to procrastinate on those difficult tasks that, in the long run, will make a positive difference in our personal productivity.

If you find that you have fluffed, then you must quickly learn from it. Take absolute responsibility. Identify what really messed you up. Don't give up on the pursuit of your goals! Make adjustments, learn from your mistakes, and decide to make the next day a much better one!

ABOUT THE AUTHOR

Ngozi Muoneke, an accomplished Cosmetic Formulator, multiple award-winning Entrepreneur, Mentor, Author and Public Speaker from London, United Kingdom, is happily married with four children of various ages.

She has extensive skills and experience in the Pharmaceutical and Cosmetic Industry. She also co-owns a cosmetics business along with her husband. Ngozi worked at the renowned Guys & St Thomas' Hospital as a Registered Specialist Aseptic Pharmacy Technician and is a member of IFSCC (International Federation of Societies of Cosmetic Chemists, SCS (Society of Cosmetic Scientists) and ILM (Institute of Leadership & Management).

Ngozi has been featured in newspapers and has written an article for the "Newham Recorder" and "Chica Business" magazine and has received awards from Be Mogul, BIS (British Invention Society) and GWINN (Global Women Inventors & Innovators Network).
Instagram: @ngozi.muoneke
Twitter: @ngozi_m

NGOZI MUONEKE

REFERENCES

"Productivity Handbook"- **Dr. Donald E. Wetmore**
"Time Management God's Way - **Craig Groeschel,**
Money Crashers" **- David Bakke**
Time Management – Goodreads.com - **Marc Mancini**
Goodreads.com - **Carl Sandberg**
"Christian time Management" **- Mike Bennett**
"Lighten Up" - **Michelle Passoff**
Photographer -**Marachi Muoneke**
Goodreads.com **- Victor Hugo**
http://www.preceptausin.org – **Live wisely: Redeem the time.**